# TAO
# CHING

## ADAPTED FOR THE CONTEMPORARY READER BY JAMES HARRIS

# LAO TZU

ISBN: 9798565443721

# DEDICATION

To the conscious awareness interpreting these words; this is more than reading and writing; this is an exchange of energy. Each of my books either highlights a void of energy; misplaced, or latent energy; and acts as a vessel to fill, replace, or invoke mental resonance with the meaning it attempts to convey. I am not simply a word specialist; language is my tool to create paradigm shifts. Each of us holds our own unique paradigm that changes throughout our life; some end up with the wealth paradigm: others the misery paradigm. This is down to the energy they receive from an external environment; but how many people are exposed to a reality creating a paradigm that benefits their life? I aim to bring you in unity with meaningful messages; which without these unique combinations of words would not otherwise be known. I hope these messages will be received by all and passed on to others.

# TABLE OF CONTENTS

# ACKNOWLEDGMENTS

I thank life for teaching me so many valuable lessons along the way. Each moment of reality, which has entered my perception, shaped and molded the character that has written this book today. Since entering this state of existence through the miracle known as birth, my internal state has been constantly growing and adapting to an external environment which has triggered a range of thoughts, feelings, and emotions. The reality I call life consists of too many people and experiences to name and explain individually, so my dedication is to all the individuals and events in my life that have given me the depth of character to write.

Thank you.

# INTRODUCTION

There are various translations of the Tao Te Ching - The Way of the Tao, also known as The Way of the Dao, Daodejing, or Dao De Jing, one of the most profound spiritual books ever to be written thousands of years ago by a sage known as Lao Tzu/Lao Tse or as some refer to him as Laozi.

The beauty of the book is that it is left open to interpretation, in your own way, as you read. The problem with this however, is that most are unable to comprehend the deeply hidden meanings of the paragraphs and form any sense from them. Whilst the book is highly enlightening to some, it is equally confusing to others.

This version contains the translation of the ancient Chinese text, and then goes on to give a unique explanation, which offers clarification on the meanings of every paragraph. Each interpretation aims to make the Tao Te Ching a lot more understandable and enjoyable for all.

The unique interpretations should allow those who are unable to grasp the wisdom from this ancient book, the opportunity to see clearly the obscured meanings cloaked within the profound paragraphs. Prepare yourself for an internal shift, as the words in this book change your perceptions on reality.

All the mystical paradoxes will be explained. Each of the 81 passages dissected for your awakening. Enjoy the following pages and let the words sooth your soul.

## ONE

The Tao that can be named is not the eternal Tao. The name that can be named is not the eternal name. The nameless is the beginning of heaven and Earth. The named is the mother of the ten thousand things. Ever desire-less, one can see the mystery. Ever desiring, one sees only the manifestations. These two spring from the same source but differ in name; this appears as darkness. Darkness within darkness. The gate to all mystery.

**Interpretation**

Lao Tzu named it Tao, for the sake of giving it a name, only in an attempt to express his perception of reality. However paradoxically, he also suggests that there is no way to name 'it', as naming something only applies to objects or actions we can see.

Anything named has been witnessed with the eye, and then labeled with a word, which we then use to communicate with others. The ten thousand things as Lao Tzu describes them, are the objects we have labeled, which without words, would not be separate entities, but fully one with all.

Without naming anything we become one with all. When we desire external objects, our psyche is filled with thoughts around acquiring that which we have labeled. This clouds the mind, and does not allow one to see the true mystery (Tao/Nature). To be desire-less, we can appreciate the mystery in all things. We can observe them without a need to possess them.

The external world which we have disintegrated into thousands upon thousands of objects by labeling, springs from the same source as heaven and earth

(Tao) but moves in an opposite direction, why? Because the external world is seen and labeled with the eye, but the internal world is darkness. When you close your eyes you go inside, you no longer see the external world and begin to feel one with all. This is the gate to all mystery.

## TWO

Under heaven all can see beauty as beauty only because there is ugliness. All can know good as good only because there is evil. Therefore having and not having arise together. Difficult and easy complement each other. Long and short contrast each other. High and low rest upon each other. Front and back follow one another. Therefore the sage goes about doing nothing, teaching no-talking. The ten thousand things rise and fall without cease. Working, yet not taking credit. Work is done then forgotten. Therefore it lasts forever.

**Interpretation**

When we attach a label to something externally we automatically create an opposite. Nothing in our external reality exists without its counterpart. You cannot have one without the other. The moment you express an opinion on something you are suggesting it is either good or bad, right or wrong. If you say 'this is good' then you will know of an opposite scenario which you would define as bad. All opposites are attached to the external environment – the ten thousand things as Lao Tzu describes them.

This paragraph suggests that the sage goes about teaching no-talking, because speech is the beginning of labeling opposites. The rise and fall relates to experiencing both of the opposites throughout your life continuously. There are no ups without downs and vice versa. All thought is based on opposites, you cannot think without an opposite. Love/Hate, Pleasure/Pain, Good/Bad, Short/Tall, Skinny/Fat are the opposite sides of the same coin.

Detach yourself from the thinking mind which is language based, and you will be able to see the opposites from a distance, becoming less affected by them personally.

# THREE

Not exalting the gifted prevents quarreling. Not collecting treasures prevents stealing. Not seeing desirable things prevents confusion of the heart. The wise therefore rule by emptying hearts and stuffing bellies, by weakening ambitions and strengthening bones. If men lack knowledge and desire, then clever people will not try to interfere. If nothing is done, then all will be well.

## Interpretation

If we choose to esteem some people higher than others, we create arguments, for exalting the gifted boosts their ego, whilst making others feel inferior. If we esteem others higher than ourselves, we create internal pain.

When placing a value on something this creates yet another comparison, which takes us away from the Tao. To value objects creates desire in others, which will cause some who are unable to obtain the object to go to inappropriate lengths to get it.

If objects were not given value by anyone, stealing would cease. The hoarder would not feel threatened and scared to lose any items, and the person who desires the object would not consider becoming a thief to get it.

If we do not desire to be or want anything, we strengthen our heart. Desiring external objects to which we then attach our sense of self is only taking us out of our inner awareness. For example, you are you without any object attached to you. When you say "this is my car," or "this is my house," you are attaching these external items to your being, and the more you accumulate mentally, the less and less you know yourself - the self which lies underneath all of the external attachments.

Emptying hearts refers to weakening desire for external objects and stuffing bellies is to make the self-full. To become more whole, by weakening the ambition to possess external objects, praise, credit etc. we strengthen our bones, i.e. ourselves.

When men have knowledge of the external world they desire, and this causes those who want to possess as much as possible to interfere with you. For example, when you have knowledge of the external world, corporations can create desire in people. They lure you into a fantasy, and bring you to forget who you are. Instead they lead you to want what they dangle in front of your eyes.

Once we empty our minds of all desire we can become free of being enticed by the knowledgeable. Even this word 'free' brings about its comparison to be trapped. Before this knowledge was accrued, there would be no thought of either of these words - free or trapped.

## FOUR

The Tao is an empty vessel; it is used but never filled. Oh, unfathomable source of ten thousand things! Blunt the sharpness, Untangle the knot, Soften the glare, Merge with dust. Oh, hidden deep but ever present! I do not know from whence it comes. It is the forefather of the gods.

### Interpretation

The ever presence of reality surrounding us, going through us, and that which creates us never stops - it is never used up.

The analogy of the empty vessel being used but never filled, is stating that if the Tao were used like a cup, once the contents were consumed it would be over. Tao is never empty, it is always being used and renewed. Never full, never empty, but continually used. What comes out of the cup, goes back into the cup.

What is sharp becomes blunt, what is knotted will become untangled, what is glaring becomes dull, what is hidden becomes present. This suggests that once you label something you will bring about its opposite. There is no escape from the opposite, there will always be reshaping of what we perceive as form and this is endless.

## FIVE

Heaven and Earth are impartial; They see the ten thousand things as straw dogs. The wise are impartial; They see the people as straw dogs. The space between heaven and Earth is like a bellows. The shape changes but not the form; The more it moves, the more it yields. More words countless. Hold fast to the center.

**Interpretation**

The Tao has no partiality towards anything or anyone simply because partiality is one sided. This brings about opposites. Heaven and earth have no partiality toward anything; at any moment there could be an earthquake destroying millions of homes etc. There is no taught in this, there is no consideration beforehand, it just does what it does. It happens.

Straw dogs, were used as ceremonial objects in ancient China. Once they were used they could be thrown on the floor, as if no one cared. The wise do not view others as objects which they should have partiality for. This does not mean that they treat people badly or favorably, they simply do not lean in either direction. To favor or have partiality for one, would mean we disfavor others.

What is meant by heaven, is the sky, when looking up we see the vastness. The space between what we see and the earth which we stand on, is like a bellows. Like a bellows which has two handles, one at the top and one at the bottom; when you open and close it, the shape of the bellows is always changing, yet to open and close it, you use the same form.

What we perceive as reality is always changing, yet the form with which it changes, is constant. The more the form continues the more it creates, as it is endless. The same can be said for us, the more we move in the same form, the more we yield.

The more words we use the less we know about what lies underneath the intellectual thinking mind, all the external words, which have been attached to objects that conjure images in our internal psyche, create our unique perception of reality. The more we speak, learn and do the more this circle of perception grows.

Stay centered in yourself. Stick to the middle of all opposites, do not seek extremes of anything, because you will encounter the opposite eventually. Stay neutral. The center is also now, do not venture into the past or future.

# SIX

The valley spirit never dies; It is the woman, primal mother. Her gateway is the root of heaven and Earth. It is like a veil barely seen. Use it; it will never fail.

## Interpretation

The valley spirit means to have a spirit close to the beginning of consciousness. The spirit of one who has no knowledge. A lowly spirit not covered in knowledge, words and external desire.

The gateway which we entered into this existence was the route of heaven and earth, the true mother. To stay humble in spirit we are more natural in ourselves. This spirit is barely seen once it has been veiled by inputting knowledge from the external environment. Once the veil is lifted, by emptying the mind, you gain the original spirit back, and it will never fail.

# SEVEN

Heaven and Earth last forever. Why do heaven and Earth last forever? They are unborn, So never die. The sage stays behind, thus he is ahead. He is detached, thus at one with all. Through selfless action, he attains fulfillment.

**Interpretation**

The existence we call reality is endless, why? Because there was no beginning; there was no birth so it could not die. This is a concept we are unfamiliar with usually as we believe everything that lives - dies. What can be said for something we consider not living then? A cardboard box for example? You wouldn't say it lives. It can change shape and disintegrate into the earth. It can become absorbed by something else - but it can't die because it never lived. The same can be said for all between heaven and earth – living is an illusion.

The sage stays behind thus he is ahead. Paradoxically being behind brings us closer to our true being. Those that seek external objects and desire particular experiences live in the world of form, where they'll always find an opposite.

To become rich means you will become poor, or once were poor. The problems with the world of form and opposites are endless. Those that are poor complain they don't have enough to buy objects which they desire. Those that are rich are scared to lose their possessions.

The sage does not desire therefore he is behind in the external race, yet this puts him in front when it comes to being more spiritually awake. He gives through selfless action thus gains fulfillment. The act of giving and helping brings true satisfaction. Give and you shall receive - receive to give.

# EIGHT

The highest good is like water. Water gives life to the ten thousand things and does not strive. It flows in places men reject and so is like the Tao. In dwelling, be close to the land. In meditation, go deep in the heart. In dealing with others, be gentle and kind. In speech, be true. In ruling, be just. In daily life, be competent. In action, be aware of the time and the season. No fight: No blame.

## Interpretation

To be truly good – there would be no reason why you are good. The highest good is always good. Like water, which nourishes all, it has no favorites - there are no preferences. If there were, this would bring about the opposite of being bad or ill-mannered to others. Therefore the highest good doesn't favor anything or anyone, it is purely good at all times. It also doesn't try to be good - it just is.

The land is the true nature. Watch it and become like it. When meditating go deep into the heart, meaning find your true nature, one that is always loving, always kind, always good.

When dealing with others, be gentle and kind, because nothing said or done by another should provoke any other response from you.

In speech be true, meaning never tell lies, make your words match your actions. In daily life be competent, meaning give your attention and diligence to all that you do.

In action be aware of time and the season, for example, when planting food for harvest the seeds need to be sown at the right time for optimal results. The same can be said for all of your actions. Be aware of the timing. Do not force anything - let things flow naturally.

## NINE

Better to stop short than fill to the brim. Over sharpen the blade, and the edge will soon blunt. Amass a store of gold and jade, and no one can protect it. Claim wealth and titles, and disaster will follow. Retire when the work is done. This is the way of heaven.

## Interpretation

This paragraph means to stick to the middle path, never going to far and never staying idle. When keeping a fine balance we do not create an opposite. If you fill to the brim eventually it will spill, sharpening a blade eventually it becomes blunt. Even if you kept it sharp until you had eroded almost the entire blade, it will finally disappear completely. Keep storing gold and jade and you will not be able to protect it, it will be taken from you in one way or another. Claiming wealth and a title, disaster follows. Once you reach a peak, you will fall. There is no way to continually rise, without reaching the peak. This is why many celebrities fade away over time, and completely lose their mind when they notice it happening. They take drug overdoses etc. to try and experience a high again.

It is better to retire gracefully than to keep striving for more. Being in the middle someone who became famous could stay level headed. Being in the middle someone can focus on their craft as opposed to the fame and fortune.

Do a job well, but when it is done call it a day, do not over do anything. Stick to the middle - this is the way to heaven.

## TEN

Carrying body and soul and embracing the one, Can you avoid separation? Attending fully and becoming supple,can you be as a newborn baby? Washing and cleansing the primal vision, Can you be without stains? Loving all men and ruling the country, Can you be without cleverness? Opening and closing the gates of heaven, can you play the role of a woman? Understanding and being open to all things, are you able to do nothing? Giving birth and nourishing, bearing yet not possessing, working yet not taking credit, Leading yet not dominating, this is the Primal Virtue.

### Interpretation

The body and mind are intertwined, what you feel in the body you feel in the mind and vice versa. Can you avoid separation, meaning can you view your whole being as one, instead of saying "this is my body," or "this is my mind". They are one and will always be one. Each having an effect on the other. Can you attend fully? Become extremely present and bring suppleness to your body and mind. Let them both be as a new born baby. Bring yourself back to the route, which you first entered this plane of existence from. Become truly supple, do not focus on one and not the other, you need to create suppleness in the body as well as the mind simultaneously. Stretching, Yoga, Tai Ji are all good methods for bringing suppleness to the body and mind. Meditation can be used to bring calmness and clarity to the internal psyche.

To wash and cleanse your vision, means to unlearn, to renounce knowledge and worldly possessions. Can you say you have been clean, without stains? To do this brings more suppleness and childlike states of mind. You will notice that the way the world encourages you to live is not clean, and that you may have already conducted unwholesome acts because of it.

To love all and rule, means to be able to guide and help others with love, as opposed to cleverness, like lies and deceit.

Opening and closing the gates of heaven, can you play the role of a women, means to be in touch with the feminine side, to acknowledge the beauty in a true woman - the sacred feminine. To be able to understand and use some of the characteristics found in a woman, such as gentleness, kindness, affection and love.

To be open to all things and do nothing, means to be able to accept all that life brings, be present for anything but not change at the core. To be able understand and interpret anything but not react to it.

To give birth and nourish means if you chose to create something, give life to it, encourage it to grow. Start what you will continue. To bear and not possess means to hold something but not claim to possess it.

To work and not take credit, means to claim no attention for your work, to not seek satisfaction or praise - simply let it be.

If you crave credit for your work and this gives a sense of pride, the moment you receive no credit you will feel unappreciated – stay in the center.

To lead and not dominate, means to help and encourage others, but do not force your views and opinions on them. Carefully guide their steps, but do not assert dominance, this will backfire and no one will follow.

There should be no opposite, no dominance equals no submission. Those who do not stay balanced create conflict and suffering for themselves and those around them. Someone who submits to dominance feels restricted and controlled; someone who is dominant does not learn from those around as they cling to their beliefs and become inflexible. The opposite of being supple in body and mind.

## ELEVEN

Thirty spokes share the wheel's hub; it is the center hole that makes it useful. Shape clay into a pot; it is the space within that makes it useful. Cut doors and windows for a room; it is the holes which make it useful. Therefore benefit comes from what is there; usefulness from what is not there.

## Interpretation

The seen and unseen are inseparable, what is believed to have use, is not that which is useful. It is the emptiness that is useful - the things we do not see.

For example, I could use an external object to type this book, but the transposition of words from my mind to yours is unseen. Once you read the words from this page, the thoughts you have are unseen. The changes in brain chemistry are unseen.

There is no use in the tangible, it's the intangible that has use. The mobile phone is tangible, the thoughts passed through speech, radio waves, to the ears of the receiver are invisible.

Each object is a vessel for something invisible. Be aware of the manifestations of the unseen. Here lies the true usefulness, when you use an external object for an invisible purpose.

All things become useful, when they become hollow, when they allow an unseen manifestation.

Pay attention to what you don't see, as this will serve a purpose in your life. Things that are unseen are usually felt, and because they are unseen are commonly taken for granted.

# TWELVE

The five colors blind the eye. The five tones deafen the ear. The five flavors dull the taste. Racing and hunting madden the mind. Precious things lead one astray. Therefore the sage is guided by what he feels and not by what he sees. He lets go of that and chooses this.

## Interpretation

In excess anything will dull the senses. In taking anything from the external environment to overload, does not allow us to really sense anymore. Once the sense perception becomes saturated it no longer enjoys simple things.

Seeking too much is an endless pursuit which is never satisfied. The more dull the senses become the more they require to feel. Hunting for external pleasures, experiences and objects, madden the mind. This makes people do crazy things to satisfy their senses.

Considering something of an external nature to be precious can be lead one astray. The sage is guided by what he feels internally – that which is unseen. Not by what he sees externally. Nothing from the outside can guide him or lure him away from his true nature, he guides himself from within.

## THIRTEEN

Accept disgrace willingly. Accept misfortune as the human condition. What do you mean by "Accept disgrace willingly"? Accept being unimportant. Do not be concerned with loss or gain. This is called "accepting disgrace willingly." What do you mean by "Accept misfortune as the human condition"? Misfortune comes from having a body. Without a body, how could there be misfortune? Surrender yourself humbly; then you can be trusted to care for all things. Love the world as your own self; then you can truly care for all things.

## Interpretation

Do not be concerned with making a name for yourself, keep yourself quiet and humble. Do not seek fame and fortune, accept yourself as you are. Be content with being unknown. Those that seek to be known for something, either succeed and then fall from the peak, or never get there and become unsatisfied.

Stay in the middle and do not seek, just be as you are. Accept misfortune as a normal occurrence and do not allow it to be considered as a negative condition. If you consider something as misfortune, then you believe there is fortune. This brings a wish to be fortunate and avoid unfortunate events. Accept misfortune means to accept both ups and downs, and not to hold on to either.

Misfortune comes from seeing yourself as a separate entity (some-body), without a body, there could be no misfortune. The essential building blocks which give life to the body, are the same in everything we see in our external reality - we are literally looking at ourselves. Those occurrences we call negatives, are purely natural, like waves crashing on top of one another, the water underneath does not say "why me," or "this is bad, the water just landed on me," it is simply neutral.

Believing we are separate makes us feel signaled out, as if we have been targeted. Everything is as it is, there is no need to attach to either a negative or a positive.

Surrender yourself and realize everything is one, then you can be trusted to care for all things – as you realize what you do to another, you do to yourself. Love everyone and everything as you are one with it, and you will truly care for all things. Because you are loving yourself. There is a reason for the saying "One Love".

## FOURTEEN

Look, it cannot be seen - it is beyond form. Listen, it cannot be heard - it is beyond sound. Grasp, it cannot be held - it is intangible. These three are indefinable; Therefore they are joined in one. From above it is not bright; From below it is not dark: An unbroken thread beyond description. It returns to nothingness. The form of the formless, The image of the imageless, It is called indefinable and beyond imagination. Stand before it and there is no beginning. Follow it and there is no end. Stay with the ancient Tao, Move with the present. Knowing the ancient beginning is the essence of Tao.

**Interpretation**

To view the outside world and perceive separation from it, further disconnects you from being at one with the Tao. Too many images lodged in the psyche, which either replay memories, or create internal visions, force detachment from the present moment.

The same can be said for hearing. Ingest too many words and sounds which repeat internally and we cannot be present with the Tao. You cannot hold the Tao, it is forever moving, reforming, changing shape. It cannot be stopped, it is intangible and nothing can hold it.

The Tao which similarly rhymes with now, the present, is all that there is. There is no way to capture the now, for once you try it has eluded you. It slips through your fingers yet it always remains there.

Sound and image accompany the Tao. They sprout from the Tao. They too cannot be held by you. You cannot capture the light, or the sound you hear. They are purely manifestations of the Tao in a single moment. Therefore sound, image and the Tao are one.

The Tao is an unbroken thread, the now we experience is always there, always has been and always will be. There is no way to truly describe it. Using words to describe it is impossible, as it is outside the realm of language. The form is formless and the image is imageless, because they are never static. No external image or sound stays the same.

Believing you can be ahead of it, you will see there is no end. You cannot view the future or stand in the future and look back. There is no end to even call anything a future, it will always be present.

Is the past real? where are you at that moment? In the present. There is no beginning, the past moment is not there. The continuing unbroken loop which is always changing, never stays the same, no beginning, no end and is impossible to capture.

Stay with the present, leave what you believe as the past and the future out of your mind. Do not keep them internally inside you. Reside with the Tao, stay in the present at all times. The present is always renewed and offers a fresh start every moment. This is the essence of Tao.

## FIFTEEN

The ancient masters were subtle, mysterious, profound and responsive. The depth of their knowledge is unfathomable. Because it is unfathomable, all we can do is describe their appearance. Watchful, like men crossing a winter stream. Alert, like men aware of danger. Courteous, like visiting guests. Yielding like ice about to melt. Simple, like un-carved blocks of wood. Hollow, like caves. Opaque, like muddy pools. Who can wait quietly while the mud settles? Who can remain still until the moment of action? Observers of the Tao do not seek fulfillment. Not seeking fulfillment, they are not swayed by desire for change.

## Interpretation

The ancient masters had unfathomable wisdom, and were subtle, mysterious and profound. The reason we can only describe their appearance, is because being aware of the Tao - they did not speak. Their wisdom was so deep, they knew that words held no importance. Therefore all one could do was observe their actions. Being watchful and alert, means they were very present, and careful in their actions, by staying one with the present moment and not rushing ahead in thought. Yielding meaning they flowed nicely with each moment, not resisting anything and accepting everything that became part of their reality. Hollow meaning they were empty of thought, which gave them the ability to be present, by not having any internal dialogue, image or perception to distort their vision of the present moment. Opaque, meaning they were not see through, you couldn't understand them, they would not talk or give much away.

To wait until the mud settles, is to have patience. Not to force anything at any given time, but to wait patiently as all things change naturally.

If you shake up a glass of water with mud in it, nothing you do to it will make it become clear again, unless you leave it alone and wait patiently. The same can be said for life, wait patiently, do not force change. Take opportunities as they present themselves, do not force them.

As the sage is desire-less, there is no care for a change, or to see specific outcomes. Allow everything to be as it is and evolve naturally. Again this applies to constant thinking. Allow the mind to settle and become quiet, watch it patiently and eventually it becomes still.

## SIXTEEN

Empty yourself of everything. Let the mind become still. The ten thousand things rise and fall while the Self watches it's return. They grow and flourish and then return to the source. Returning to the source is stillness, which is the way of nature. The way of nature is unchanging. Knowing constancy is insight. Not knowing constancy leads to disaster. Knowing constancy, the mind is open. With an open mind, you will be openhearted. Being openhearted, you will act royally. Being royal, you will attain the divine. Being divine, you will be at one with the Tao. Being at one with the Tao is eternal. And though the body fades, the Tao will never pass away.

## Interpretation

Unlearn and let go of all thought. Stay present, let the mind become settled, and in this state you will view external objects around you without forming attachment. You return to your source, the Tao. You grow and flourish in this state, as you are now one with your natural being.

In this stillness of mind, you are one with nature. The way of nature does not change, it is natural. It does not struggle to become something it is not, it doesn't favor outcomes - it is simply being.

Constancy is another word for unchanging, or commitment. Commitment is to remain the same in a particular aspect. Understanding constancy is insight, which means that when we commit to something, without struggling, we allow the power of the Tao to create the change slowly. Just as a tree grows into a mighty oak over years, very slowly over time. Knowing constancy/commitment is insight. Not knowing constancy or commitment to anything we never achieve greatness in anything in particular.

Understanding the concept of constancy, we can achieve great things, without force or struggle, by simply being one with the Tao at all times.

Knowing constancy opens the mind, when the mind is open the heart becomes open. When your heart is open, you act royally, with great presence in everything you do and with everyone you meet. Being royal you will attain divinity. Being divine you are at one with the Tao. Being one with the Tao is eternal. Knowing that the body is purely a vessel of consciousness, you understand that when the body dissolves, the essence of you remains with the Tao. Nothing leaves the Tao and the Tao never dies - you are therefore eternal.

## SEVENTEEN

The very highest leader is barely known. Then comes that which people know and love. Then that which is feared. Then that which is despised. Who does not trust enough will not be trusted. When actions are performedwithout unnecessary speech, the people say, "we did it!"

**Interpretation**

The highest leader is the one who does not select himself as the leader, because the leader leads without the people knowing he is leading. He or she leads by example - without words. He/she needs no speech to prompt actions from anyone. The leader leads himself well, and those around follow.

Next is someone that the people love, they follow because they love him or her. They are very close to that person and follow purely by being around them.

Next is a leader who is feared. The people follow by being inflicted with fear, and act due to being scared.

Finally one who is despised, the people who form hate for another person will act out of hate. Those who do not trust enough, are those to be distrusted, the predominant thoughts of distrust are of their own character.

When the highest leader leads, he or she takes no credit, they lead by example and need no recognition by anyone, therefore those around hardly feel his or her input, and believe they did it themselves. Lead without talking, set an example.

## EIGHTEEN

When the great Tao is forgotten, kindness and morality arise. When wisdom and intelligence are born, the great pretense begins. When there is no peace within the family, filial piety and devotion arise. When the country is confused and in chaos, loyal ministers appear.

**Interpretation**

Being one with the present moment you allow all to be as it is, there is no intellectual thought or attachment to right or wrong, good or bad. When presence is forgotten people act kind and moral, wisdom and intelligence start the great pretense, which means the great act. When the Tao is forgotten everyone begins to "act" and tries to be someone. Acting arises from a false sense of self and time perception which veils all present moments – The sage does not try or act. The sage simply is one with nature, not the external environment.

When there is no peace with-in a family, filial piety and devotion arise, meaning that when the Tao is forgotten the comparisons are active again, there will be moments of non-peace, then moments of cohesion. When the country is in chaos, loyal ministers appear, as there is chaos ministers appear to calm the chaos, there is always an opposite, and what this paragraph is saying is that being one with the Toa is to stay in the middle. Be the balance, be the in-between. When this is forgotten and we slip into comparison, either side, we create the opposite affect eventually.

## NINETEEN

Give up sainthood, renounce wisdom, and it will be a hundred times better for everyone. Give up kindness, renounce morality, and men will rediscover filial piety and love. Give up ingenuity, renounce profit, and bandits and thieves will disappear. These three are outward forms alone; they are not sufficient in themselves. It is more important to see the simplicity, to realize one's true nature, to cast off selfishness and temper desire.

**Interpretation**

When those believe they are wise, or saintly, when they display these qualities to those around, it makes others feel inadequate, this leads to problems in what we call society, we create disparity amongst the people. Give up holding on to the labels we attach to ourselves, including sainthood, wisdom, kindness and morality, and each person would return to their source. They will love their mother, and family loyalty will reappear, instead of those feeling inadequate leaving the family to become what they see others act as.

When we hold on to something we create the opposite, by holding on to sainthood, wisdom, kindness and morality, we bring about the opposite. Stick to the middle, be nothing, be no-one. If all gave up profiteering, thieves will disappear, because you create in those that don't have, the desire to have. When they can't have, some with intense desire will rob and steal, lie and cheat to get what they want. If no one desired these things, and no one paraded them as though they were of importance, no one would take notice and care. No one would struggle and strain to attain anything. However these are outward forms, meaning that they require someone else to change, to not create desire in someone else, but, it is of more importance, for one to temper their own desire and cast off any selfish qualities. By doing this, what others do will not have any effect, you will not care for what others do, and realize your own true nature.

# TWENTY

Give up learning, and put an end to your troubles. Is there a difference between yes and no? Is there a difference between good and evil? Must I fear what others fear? What nonsense! Other people are contented, enjoying the sacrificial feast of the ox. In spring some go to the park, and climb the terrace, but I alone am drifting, not knowing where I am. Like a newborn baby before it learns to smile, I am alone, without a place to go. Others have more than they need, but I alone have nothing. I am a fool. Oh, yes! I am confused. Others are clear and bright, but I alone am dim and weak. Others are sharp and clever, but I alone am dull and stupid. Oh, I drift like the waves of the sea, without direction, like the restless wind. Everyone else is busy, but I alone am

aimless. I am different. I am nourished by
the great mother.


**Interpretation**

Learning is to accumulate knowledge,
thoughts, visions, intellectual capability.
To let go of learning is to simply be with
the present moment at all times, and give
up creating a separation from yourself.
Imagine your mind being divided in two,
one side is to contain all the knowledge
you put into it. However it is the other
side, which is the true you, the you that
was there before the split occurred. The
consciousness drifts into the side, which
holds the knowledge and finds it difficult
to go back into the side which contains
your true being. Let go of thoughts and
knowledge to discover your true being
again. Without knowledge there is no
difference between yes and no, good and
evil. When you use your thinking

intellectual mind, you can create fear, the opposite of what you would like to see happen, Lao Tzu was suggesting that he has no room internally for thoughts which are only going to give rise to fear. He does not need to be like everyone else.

There are those that feel contented only when feasting, what happens when they run out of substance to consume? The will not feel content anymore. There are those that seek activities that they believe bring enjoyment, yet cannot be content when the activities are over. To drift not knowing where you are, is to be content at all times, not in external pleasures and desires, simply to be content with the situation as it is, to drift aimlessly in whatever direction the wind blows. Like a new born baby before it learns to smile, I am alone with no place to go, is the state in which a baby cannot see externally and cannot move for itself, Lao Tzu is suggesting to be in a similar state to this, not to take in from the external environment and to not force movement in any direction, just be as you are.

Some people have more than they need, but it is better to have nothing at all, because those that cling to worldly possession, are psychological hoarders, who need more and more to be satisfied. Holding on to nothing, to have nothing and being content, brings no problems, you create no opposite for yourself. To simply not have, and not care, there is no opposite, no desire for more.

I am a fool, I am confused, others are bright, I am dim and weak, others are sharp and clever, I am dull and stupid, means Lao Tzu had either emptied his mind of all desire, or never had any desire in the first place. Either way, he was suggesting to renounce all desire and lose knowledge, others may consider him stupid, dull and weak etc., but he did not care. While others are confined by thought and desire, he can be empty and drift aimlessly like waves of the sea, in any direction. While everyone is busy seeking something externally, Lao Tzu suggests being nourished by the great mother, the Tao, the Earth.

## TWENTY-ONE

The greatest Virtue is to follow Tao and Tao alone. The Tao is elusive and intangible. Oh, it is intangible and elusive, and yet within is image.Oh, it is elusive and intangible, and yet within is form. Oh, it is dim and dark, and yet within is essence. This essence is very real, and therein lies faith. From the very beginning until now its name has never been forgotten. Thus I perceive the creation. How do I know the ways of creation? Because of this.

**Interpretation**

To follow the Tao means to be at one with the moment, there is no tomorrow, there is no yesterday, there will only be the present. Although it is impossible to pause reality, to stay at one with the present is no easy task, as the present is forever changing. Staying one with the Tao, is to flow with each moment of reality naturally without struggle. Through our eyes we can see an image in front of us, but it is forever changing, thus it is elusive. It is elusive and intangible, yet there appears to be solid forms in front of us, which we can reach out and touch, however our so called solid surroundings are always changing. The surroundings are reflections of light, the colors cannot be captured, yet they are the essence of what we see. What we see is very alive, and that's what gives us faith that it is real.

From the very beginning until now, the Tao has never been forgotten, meaning it has always been the only thing that has ever been. It is eternal. Because we can see these forms in front of us, we can witness the creation. We are part of the Tao and are able to witness the creations caused by the movement of the Tao. We witness ourselves create.

## TWENTY-TWO

Yield and overcome; bend and be straight; empty and be full; wear out and be new; have little and gain; have much and be confused. Therefore the wise embrace the one, and set an example to all. Not putting on a display, they shine forth. Not justifying themselves, they are distinguished. Not boasting, they receive recognition. Not bragging, they never falter. They do not quarrel, so no one quarrels with them. Therefore the ancients say, "Yield and overcome." Is that an empty saying? Be really whole, and all things will come to you.

**Interpretation**

Do not resist what happens during your lifetime, flow with life, let things be as they are, do not offer any struggle. To bend and be straight means to be flexible and follow the Tao, like a tree in the wind, it simply bends in whichever direction the wind blows. Something that is lifeless, is considered to be static, inflexible and rigid. Similarly if a tree was rigid when a strong wind blows, it will snap.

Become empty and be full. Means to empty the mind, of all thoughts and let your natural energy take its place. Imagine a bowl of water, if you put many objects into the bowl, it will spill. This is the same with too many thoughts in the mind, if we start to remove the objects from the bowl of water (thoughts from the mind) the water level goes back to its natural state, as does the mind when unnecessary thoughts are removed.

To have little in terms of material possessions, we gain more internally. Because the more we attach our sense of self to external possessions, the less we are in touch with our true essence. If you have too much, you become confused, and are continually seeking more and more. There is no end to gathering material possessions, and the more you label as part of your identity, the less you can see the true you, which resides underneath the attachments.

The wise embrace the Tao, knowing that nothing externally belongs to them, they set an example for all to follow. Not an example based on ego and material possessions. A true example, of being completely whole. In doing this they shine brighter than those who possess more external objects, because what they possess internally shines through their being. They do not justify themselves to anyone, they simply follow the Tao, they appear distinguished to those around. Without boasting, people recognize their accomplishments, and as they do not brag, they never lose their enthusiasm for what they are doing. They do not take part in arguments, as it takes two to argue, no one can argue with them.

To yield is to become fully empty of the external world, and focus purely internally. Become whole, one with nature, your true essence, and all good things will come to you, you don't need to chase anything.

# TWENTY-THREE

To talk little is natural. High winds do not last all morning. Heavy rain does not last all day. Why is this? Heaven and Earth! If heaven and Earth cannot make things eternal, How is it possible for man? He who follows the Tao Is at one with the Tao. He who is virtuous experiences virtue. He who loses the way is lost. When you are at one with the Tao, the Tao welcomes you. When you are at one with Virtue, the Virtue is always there. When you are at one with loss, the loss is experienced willingly. He who does not trust enough will not be trusted.

**Interpretation**

It is unnatural to talk all the time, if we follow the Tao, we see there is no consistent rain, no consistent wind.

Nothing continues indefinitely, so why do people talk so much? It is not natural. Heaven and earth refers to the balance, which Taoists believe in, known as Taijitu, this is the balance of all things. The symbol is a circle, with a black half and a white half, balanced further with a white dot in the black half, and a black dot in the white half. White is Yang (male) black is Yin (female). As there is balance in all things, talking consistently is considered completely unnatural and should be balanced with silence.

One who follows the Tao, is one with it. One who is virtuous, will experience what virtue brings. One who does not follow the Tao is lost, either thinking of past or future, and is not being completely present. At any moment if you chose to be one with the Tao the Tao is always ready to embrace you. If you are truly at one with virtue, the you will never perform un-virtuous acts, virtue does not leave you. If you are open to accept loss, then there is no resistance to it, as you embrace it willingly, you understand that loss is inevitable. Those who do not trust enough, will not be trusted by others, as the predominant thoughts of others, are usually self-reflections.

## TWENTY-FOUR

He who stands on tiptoe is not steady. He who strides cannot maintain the pace. He who makes a show is not enlightened. He who is self-righteous is not respected. He who boasts achieves nothing. He who brags will not endure. According to followers of the Tao, "These are extra food and unnecessary luggage." They do not bring happiness. therefore followers of the Tao avoid them.

**Interpretation**

The one who is not firmly grounded, is always off balance. Standing on tip toe is to be completely lost and out of sync with the Tao. He who is routed in the present is solid.

To stride, is to rush and run out of energy. Those without patience, will rush to see a change. This change will not happen quick enough for them so they will run out of motivation. All things take time and the way of nature is not fast and rushed, but slow and steady.

He who promotes his/her righteous behavior is not respected, as one who is truly righteous has no need to boast. The righteous know, that words are hollow, and are unnecessary, to be a righteous example, one must only act righteous, without speaking it.

Those who brag, clearly are only creating something for the opinions of other people. They are seeking to feel powerful, by having others praise them. These type of people are not righteous, nor are they performing any worthwhile deeds. For them their actions are a means to an end, and the more they brag, the less natural energy they have, as they believe they gain power from external perceptions, they lose their own sense of self-worth and cannot endure.

To gain anything from the external world, is additional luggage for the mind, which hinders our ability to be one with the Tao. The more internal perceptions we have based on our external environment, the less we are in touch with the Tao. This does not create happiness, therefore perceptions are best to be avoided. Focus purely on now.

## TWENTY-FIVE

Something mysteriously formed, born before heaven and earth. In the silence and the void, standing alone and unchanging, ever present and in motion. perhaps it is the mother of ten thousand things. I do not know its name - call it Tao. For lack of a better word, I call it great. Being great, it flows far away. Having gone far, it returns. Therefore, "Tao is great; Heaven is great; Earth is great; The king is also great. "These are the FOUR great powers of the universe, and the king is one of them. Man follows Earth. Earth follows heaven. Heaven follows the Tao. Tao follows what is natural.

**Interpretation**

The Tao is mysteriously formed, born before what we called heaven and earth, it was always there. In silence and in emptiness, it stands alone and is unchanging. Although the forms around us change, the Tao is always present and never changes. It always has been and will never end. It is the ten thousand things as Lao Tzu calls them, which means the never ending amount of objects around us, which once named, creates the disintegration of the whole. The Tao being the whole, cannot be named, to name it would to be to view it as an object. It is purely called Tao to point to it, however it cannot be labeled with words. As it is whole, everything makes up the Tao in each moment of reality.

The Tao is great and flows far and returns. It continuously changes, reforming and reshaping, to be completely still one can feel in alignment with the Tao.

The Tao, Heaven, Earth and the King are great. A King is great because he follows the earth, the earth is great because it follows heaven (godly essence) and Heaven is great because it is always one with the Tao. The Tao is supreme, as it always follows itself, which is purely natural. Therefore the king, can indirectly follow the Tao, by watching and observing the closest thing in out externally perception which embodies the nature of the Tao, which is the Earth. The Earth is heavenly, it flows, rises and falls in perfect harmony and balance. All that is heavenly follows the Tao.

## TWENTY-SIX

The heavy is the root of the light. The still is the master of unrest. Therefore the sage, traveling all day, Does not lose sight of his baggage. Though there are beautiful things to be seen, He remains unattached and calm. Why should the lord of ten thousand chariots act lightly in public? To be light is to lose one's root. To be restless is to lose one's control.

**Interpretation**

What is heavy, is routed and not easy to move. To be still is to master the unrest. The internal commotion can be relieved by silencing the mind and becoming completely still. To be still one can be whole with the Tao. The sage who travels through the day, does not lose sight of his baggage, this is the only baggage he wishes to hold, which are his virtues, and that which matters. There are many temptations, yet to be dethatched from wanting anything beyond our inner self we remain calm. Why should he act this way? Because heaviness is the route of the light, his focus is heavy internally, if he were light, he can easily be moved by temptation and external desires. If he is restless in thought, he does not own his mind and lacks self-control. One should be firmly rooted in virtue, and completely at peace in the mind.

## TWENTY-SEVEN

A good walker leaves no tracks; a good speaker makes no slips; a good reckoner needs no tally. A good door needs no lock, yet no one can open it. Good binding requires no knots, yet no one can loosen it. Therefore the sage takes care of all men and abandons no one. He takes care of all things and abandons nothing. This is called "following the light." What is a good man? A teacher of a bad man. What is a bad man? A good man's lesson. If the teacher is not respected, and the student not cared for, confusion will arise, however clever one is. This is the crux of mystery.

## Interpretation

A skillful person does not create unskillful acts. The sage, pays attention to detail, and does things as they should be done, in no rush, to achieve perfection. A skillful person also nourishes all those he/she communicates with, is always open to help and does not turn his/her back on anyone. A good person has a lot to teach a bad person, and also learn from them at the same time. A good person is a role model for a bad person, whilst the good person learns and becomes even greater simply by observing the bad. If the teacher is not respected by the bad person, or the bad person not cared for, this creates confusion, as the bad person is not learning from the good person, and the good person is becoming bad by not caring for the bad person. This point should be well observed and is crucial to becoming a master.

## TWENTY-EIGHT

Know the strength of man, but keep a woman's care! Be the stream of the universe! Being the stream of the universe, ever true and unswerving, become as a little child once more. Know the white, but keep the black! Be an example to the world! Being an example to the world, ever true and unwavering, return to the infinite. Know honor, yet keep humility. Be the valley of the universe! Being the valley of the universe, Ever true and resourceful, return to the state of the un-carved block. When the block is carved, it becomes useful. When the sage uses it, he becomes the ruler. Thus, "A great tailor cuts little."

## Interpretation

Know the opposites, and keep both with you. To have the strength of a man, for a man is encouraged, however to know that there is a balance of masculine and feminine in all. Understand the qualities of a woman, and respect them. Know the Yin (Female), but keep the Yang (Male). For a woman Know the Yang (Male) but keep the Yin (Female). If we flow like a stream from A-B without effort, without trying to control the direction and simply going with the flow, we become child-like again. The times when we were not burdened with thought. Know the bad, but keep the good. Be true, and do not deviate from this path and return to the infinite.

Know honor and have great self-esteem, but with it keep humility, do not boast about your work. Be the valley of the universe, be the resourceful one, however return to your natural state, when you are not working. Become natural in yourself, the underlying presence which comes before being molded by the external world. Only use your resources when you need to. When becoming useful, take great care of the work you produce, be very precise. When you decide to start something, leave nothing undone.

## TWENTY-NINE

Do you think you can take over the Tao and improve it? I do not believe it can be done. The Tao is sacred. You cannot improve it. If you try to change it, you will ruin it. If you try to hold it, you will lose it. So sometimes things are ahead and sometimes they are behind; sometimes breathing is hard, sometimes it comes easily; sometimes there is strength and sometimes weakness; sometimes one is up and sometimes down. Therefore the sage avoids extremes, excesses, and complacency.

**Interpretation**

You cannot improve or control the Tao, it cannot be done. The Tao is sacred, to try to change it means to force a direction in reality. This will only backfire, and not work in your favor. That which you try to hold on to, you will lose. Sometimes, things are up sometimes they are down, something's are hard, while others are easy, and all these things eventually change. This is the nature of the Tao, so the sage endeavors to stay centered, and avoids extremes and excess of anything. To have little, one craves more, to have a lot one fears losing it. The sage stays centered, if he finds himself in an extreme position, he will not be complacent as he knows this will change.

# THIRTY

Whenever you advise a ruler in the way of the Tao, counsel him not to use force to conquer the Tao. For this would only cause resistance. Thorn bushes spring up wherever the army has passed. Lean years against the wake of a great war. Just do what needs to be done. Never take advantage of power. Achieve results, but never glory in them. Achieve results, but never boast. Achieve results, but never be proud. Achieve results, because this is the natural way. Achieve results, but not through violence. Force is followed by loss of strength. This is not the way of the Tao. That which goes against the Tao comes to an early end.

## Interpretation

To conquer the Tao, is to become one with it, there is no force that can prevail against the Tao, this only causes resistance. When advising others about their journey in life, advise the follow the Tao, without force. Thorn bushes spring up where the army has passed, means that those who move with force, leave thorny paths, which remain for many years. Do not use force in life, only do what needs to be done, no more. If you find yourself in power, do not take advantage of it, as this is using force and will only leave trails of thorns. Aim for results, not glory, aim for results but do not boast, aim for results but never be proud, aim for results but not through force. Relishing in glory, boasting and showing excess pride are characteristics which are not one with the Tao. Using force only diminishes ones strength.

Those who use force go against the Tao and their lives will be cut shorter.

## THIRTY-ONE

Good weapons are instruments of fear;
all creatures hate them. Therefore
followers of Tao never use them. The wise
man prefers the left. The man of war
prefers the right. Weapons are
instruments of fear; they are not a wise
man's tools. He uses them only when he
has no choice. Peace and quiet are dear to
his heart, and victory no cause for
rejoicing. If you rejoice in victory, then
you delight in killing; If you delight in
killing, you cannot fulfill yourself. On
happy occasions precedence is given to
the left, On sad occasions to the right. In
the army the general stands on the left,
The commander-in-chief on the right.
This means that war is conducted like a
funeral. When many people are being
killed, They should be mourned in

heartfelt sorrow. That is why a victory must be observed like a funeral.

## Interpretation

No sentient being welcomes violence, and understands that weapons are tools which are used for violent acts. Those who follow the Tao, know not to cause violence and fear in others. Those that understand this, stay with the Tao, those who don't, stay on the outside. Weapons are not a wise man's instruments. He may only use them if absolutely necessary and under any circumstances does not like to do so. He does not rejoice in harming another, it does not bring fulfillment. On happy occasions, those with the Tao will win any war. On sad occasions those not in alignment with the Tao will kill. Those with the Tao that are forced to kill, view this act like a funeral, with great sorrow.

## THIRTY-TWO

The Tao is forever undefined. Small though it is in the unformed state, it cannot be grasped. If kings and lords could harness it, the ten thousand things would come together and gentle rain fall. Men would need no more instruction and all things would take their course. Once the whole is divided, the parts need names. There are already enough names. One must know when to stop. Knowing when to stop averts trouble. Tao in the world is like a river flowing home to the sea.

**Interpretation**

There is no absolute definition for the Tao, to define means to label with words, which cannot be done. Words are used to create a thought, and the Tao cannot be captured by thought. To know the Tao is to be one with it. If people could understand the Tao, then all things would become one. There would be no more separation with the use of words. There would be no more guidance, and all things would flow naturally. Everything is whole, but once divided with words, it becomes hard for the internal psyche to understand there is no separation. There are too many words, and one needs to know when to stop using them, and to limit their use as often as possible. This turns away trouble. To be at one with the Tao, is like a river returning to the sea, once you become one with it you return to the source. Simply meaning that we have separated ourselves from the whole, into fragments, and to return is to become part of the great source, and to be whole again.

## THIRTY-THREE

Knowing others is wisdom; knowing the self is enlightenment. Mastering others requires force; mastering the self needs strength. He who knows he has enough is rich. Perseverance is a sign of willpower. He who stays where he is endures. To die but not to perish is to be eternally present.

## Interpretation

To know others, we can gain wisdom from their actions without having to complete the actions ourselves. We can become truly wise, simply by observing the behaviors in others. To know thyself is enlightenment, as one can fully self-reflect on how and why we have come to act and behave in the ways we do. We can start to alter ourselves to remove unwanted qualities and preserve virtues that serve us well.

To master other people, requires force, to manipulate goes against the Tao, as all things should take their course naturally. Mastering thyself, requires the greatest of strength, as we live in a world which has taken us into a fantasy reality which is not one with the Tao. To master oneself is to return to the source, this requires great strength against the external forces on the psyche.

To know you have enough, is to be content. He who is content is always rich, as he does not perceive a lack in anything. He no longer seeks external objects to give him/her a sense of worth/wealth.

To persevere shows great will power, which is the great force that is required to master one self. Perseverance should be used to stay on track with that which we truly want. If you stay where you are, and preserve you endure. To fully understand that death will be in a present moment, is to die before you die, and give up the external world for pleasure, as it is meaningless. This is to become fully awake in this reality, before death.

## THIRTY-FOUR

The great Tao flows everywhere, both to the left and to the right. The ten thousand things depend upon it; it holds nothing back. It fulfills its purpose silently and makes no claim. It nourishes the ten thousand things, and yet is not their lord. It has no aim; it is very small. The ten thousand things return to it, yet it is not their lord. It is very great. It does not show greatness, and is therefore truly great.

**Interpretation**

The Tao is prevalent everywhere, it flows all around us, it is the essence of everything. It is us, and the life of what we perceive as the ten thousand objects. It has no preference for anyone or anything, there is no holding back. It simply flows and nourishes all. It constantly fulfills its purpose and needs no recognition, it gives yet it is not an idol of worship, it has no purpose. The ten thousand things are part of it, yet it does not claim to own them. It does not own them, because there is no separation. It does not reveal itself and boast, therefore it is truly great, it requires no applause, or gratification. Be the same as the Tao, nourish all and crave no attention.

## THIRTY-FIVE

All men will come to him who keeps to the one, for there lie rest and happiness and peace. Passersby may stop for music and good food, but a description of the Tao seems without substance or flavor. It cannot be seen, it cannot be heard, and yet it cannot be exhausted.

## Interpretation

Those who notice the one who is centered in the Tao, will come to him/her for rest, for with him/her lies true happiness and peace. Those may walk by and not notice, because they are drawn to the pleasures of the external world, such as music and cooking, which can be alluring. The words which attempt to convey the meaning of the Tao, may seem dull, boring and flavorless because the

Tao cannot be heard or seen, yet once you are one with the Tao, it's power is inexhaustible.

# THIRTY-SIX

That which shrinks must first expand. That which fails must first be strong. That which is cast down must first be raised. Before receiving there must be giving. This is called perception of the nature of things. Soft and weak overcome hard and strong. Slow overcome the fast. Let your workings remain a mystery, just show people the results.

**Interpretation**

This paragraph highlights further, that each object of thought which is perceived in an external world, has an opposite. There is natural balance and harmony between all things. Everything has an opposite, the two opposites aren't always in correlation to good and bad. The two opposites can both be good, and both be bad at the same time. For example, if you give love, you will receive love, if you give hate, you will receive hate. Give good receive good, give bad receive bad. The opposite to good and bad exist in our external reality but whilst you are being good and receiving good, another in the world can be performing bad acts and receiving bad responses. This is the perception of nature and all things, that there is an opposite and balance of all things. Yet if we chose the balance of good, we can overcome the bad. The softest thing in the world over comes the hard - water can erode stones. When performing actions, take your time, add diligence and do things properly, regardless of how long it will take. The slow overcome the fast. Let your work remain a mystery, do not boast or brag, simply let the results speak.

## THIRTY-SEVEN

Tao abides in non-action, yet nothing is left undone. If Kings and lords observed this, the ten thousand things would develop naturally. If they still desired to act, they would return to the simplicity of formless substance. Without for there is no desire. Without desire there is and in this way all things would be at peace.

## Interpretation

The Tao is reforming and reshaping naturally, nothing is forced to be done, yet nothing is left undone. If men and women could observe this, they would allow all things to develop naturally without interference. To be at one with the Tao means to live in the present without forced action, however if one desired to act it would be with simplicity and without manipulation of the external world. There would be no desire to control events, or try to direct the Tao. Without this desire all things would find peace.

## THIRTY-EIGHT

A truly good man is not aware of his goodness, and is therefore good. A foolish man tries to be good, and is therefore is not good. A truly good man does nothing, yet leaves nothing undone. A foolish man is always doing, yet much remains to be done. When a truly kind man does something, he leaves nothing undone. When a just man does something, he leaves a great deal to be done. When a disciplinarian does something and no one responds, he rolls up his sleeves in an attempt to enforce order. Therefore when Tao is lost, there is goodness. When goodness is lost, there is kindness. When kindness is lost, there is justice. When justice is lost, there is ritual. Now ritual is the husk of faith and loyalty, the beginning of confusion. Knowledge of the future is only a flowery trapping of Tao. It is the beginning of folly. Therefore the truly great man dwells on what is real and not what is on the surface, on the fruit and not the flower. Therefore accepting one and rejecting the other.

### Interpretation

Those that are truly good, are not trying to be good. This is a natural state for them. Those who have to try to be good, cannot be truly good, because to try to be good, means they must know they are bad. A truly good man, doesn't try, therefore his goodness is never lost at any stage. The person who is trying to be good, will always leave something undone, because an act does not last. The truly good mad is always good without being aware of it.

When there is no good around, those who want to correct it will appear. When a man of discipline says something and no one listens, he tries to use force. Using force does not work, as he/she is trying to manipulate others. To master himself, and display the results as opposed to speaking - is better.

To follow the Tao, is to be like water, to truly nourish and be good to all things. When the Tao is lost, those try to be good, and when goodness is lost, there is slight kindness towards others here and there. When kindness is lost, there will be those who want to teach justice. When there is no one teaching morals, there will only be ritual, in those who have none. They will be stuck in thought patterns without change.

All rituals are the beginning of loyalty toward and faith of future outcomes. Those who are stuck in ritual are loyal to their behavior and have faith in what their actions will bring (good or bad).

However to be stuck in ritual is to contemplate the future, which is the beginning of confusion, as it is impossible to see the future. Therefore the wise do not focus on the future, only what is visible now. They focus on the present and adapt, they have no ritual based on a future outcome. They simply act in the present (with good virtues at all times).

# THIRTY-NINE

These things from ancient times arise from one: the sky is whole and clear. The earth is whole and firm. The spirit is whole and strong. The valley is whole and full. The ten thousand things are whole and alive. Kings and lords are whole, and the country is upright. All these are in virtue of wholeness. The clarity of the sky prevents its falling. The firmness of the earth prevents its splitting. The strength of the spirit prevents it being used up. The fullness of the valley prevents its running dry. The growth of the ten thousand things prevent their drying out. The leadership of kings and lords prevent the downfall of the country. Therefore the humble is the root of the noble. The low is the foundation of the high. Princes and lords consider themselves "orphaned", "widowed" and "worthless". Do they not depend on being humble? Too much success is not an advantage. Do not tinkle like jade or clatter like stone chimes.

## Interpretation

Everything in our existence which we see to date, as been there from what we perceive to be ancient times. Nothing is new, it is purely the same substance which has always been here, only it has been reshaped. The sky is whole, the earth is strong, the valleys are whole, all things are alive and belong to one. When leaders are whole, the country will be whole. All will possess the virtues of wholeness. The clarity of the sky prevents it from falling, the firmness of the earth prevents it from splitting, and the strength of the spirit prevents it from being used up, and the fullness of the valley prevents it from running dry. What this means, is that when things are whole and not interfered with, they are solid and firm. They are one with the Tao. When things are not one with the Tao, they will be a lack of completeness. The sky will be polluted, the earth will create earthquakes, the spirit of people will be unclean and unwholesome. Nothing will be in a natural order.

For things to be in order, they must be whole. Therefore being humble is the route of being noble. Being low is the foundation for the high. Too much success is not an advantage because you will not be whole, when you are high, you cannot be firmly grounded.

# FORTY

Returning is the motion of the Tao. Yielding is the way of the Tao. The ten thousand things are born of being. Being is born of not being.

## Interpretation

The nature of the Tao, is not one of struggle and strain. To be closer to the Tao, we must yield to the present moment, and be flexible. The ten thousand things in an external reality, which seem solid are created through emptiness, emptiness appears solid. They are neither there or not there. Each creates the other. The golden circle, The Tao which illuminates all, creates the perception of solid matter, however it is empty.

## FORTY-ONE

The wise student hears of the Tao and practices it diligently. The average student hears of the Tao and gives it thought now and again. The foolish student hears of the Tao and laughs aloud. If there were no laughter, the Tao would not be what it is. Hence it is said: The bright path seems dim; going forward seems like retreat; the easy way seems hard; the highest Virtue seems empty; great purity seems sullied; a wealth of Virtue seems inadequate; the strength of Virtue seems frail; real Virtue seems unreal; the perfect square has no corners; great talents ripen late; the highest notes are hard to hear; the greatest form has no shape; the Tao is hidden and without name. The Tao alone nourishes and brings everything to fulfillment.

**Interpretation**

Those who understand the Tao, will follow it diligently, as opposed to those who only contemplate it every now and then. A fool will hear about the Tao and laugh, but this again is a manifestation of the Tao in front of us. To understand the Tao is to understand ourselves. However to go into ourselves and find the Tao and to be one with the Tao, the path seems dim, because it is letting go of the external world. To gain internally is to lose externally, therefore it seems hard, but should be easier. The highest virtue seems empty, and for some it can be difficult to release the external reality. The wealth to be gained by losing attachment to the external world seems foolish, and for some is inadequate. The strength of these virtues, may appear to another as weak. These virtues seem unreal.

The perfect square has no corners, means to be rounded, and not stiff. To relax and allow the Tao to flow through you and everything. The highest notes are hard to hear, means that the greatest of perception may be hard to notice. Greatest of talent ripens late, it does not rush, it grows slowly and naturally. The greatest form, is shapeless, like the Tao it is hidden and has no name. Like a shape that has never been seen, it cannot be visualized. The Tao nourishes all.

## FORTY-TWO

The Tao begot one. One begot two. Two begot three. And three begot the ten thousand things. The ten thousand things carry yin (female) and embrace yang (male). They achieve harmony by combining these forces. Men hate to be "orphaned," "widowed," or "worthless," But this is how kings and lords describe themselves. For one gains by losing and loses by gaining. What others teach, I also teach; that is: "A violent man will die a violent death!" This will be the essence of my teaching.

### Interpretation

Now that we label objects and everything in our external perception; we split it all into pieces. Thousands and thousands of fragments, all labeled with words. We believe that all of these objects are separate, yet they all are one and come from the same source - the Tao. Everything in our external perception, carries internal energy, yin and yang (Female and Male). This energy is balanced to create harmony. When this balance is not equal, there will be disharmony. The balance can be in anything, it can be in your body, it can be between a man and a woman. There is balance in all.

Being labeled a king or lord, does not mean the standard term of a king or a lord, each individual can be a king or a lord in their own right, by understanding this book and being one with the Tao. The kings and lords, have no problem being lowly people, people who have little, because the more of the external world we attach to our being, the more we identify with external objects and possessions, the less we have internally.

So to become like a king or a lord, is to relinquish external desires and possessions.

To embrace the Tao, is also to carry it with you, to teach it to others through your actions. Not through your words. Be the embodiment of a sage, one who is always with the Tao. Be an example. A violent man will only create violence for himself. Create peace for yourself and others.

## FORTY-THREE

The softest thing in the universe overcomes the hardest thing in the universe. That without substance can enter where there is no room. Hence I know the value of non-action. Teaching without words and work without doingare understood by very few.

## Interpretation

The softest thing in the world, endures. Water can flow freely, be consumed and travel anywhere, yet it is continually recycled. Hard objects can be broken and shattered into many pieces. Water is soft and yielding. The soft overcomes the hard. Water can erode stones. Throw a stone in the water and the water simply moves out its way. Generally people believe to be soft means to be weak, yet there is great strength, energy and flexibility in the soft. Trees sway in the wind, those which are hard will snap. This is the same for those who are rigid in body and mind. The body must be kept flexible and supple, as well as the mind, we should not hold onto a thought for too long, we must let thoughts flow freely and not become trapped with the psyche on repeat. Those that can keep their body and mind supple, will be closer to being at one with the Tao.

In Taoism there is a concept known as Wu Wei, this is considered to be one of the most supreme virtues. Wu Wei, roughly translates to effortless action, or to do without doing. This does not mean to do nothing. It means to flow freely with your life, and to not force things to happen, or to rush. Not to push for particular outcomes, or try to manipulate life. This does not mean to not do anything at all, but it means to let go of the fruit and focus on planting the seeds.

Do not stress or strain yourself, trying to fit your life into a predefined box, simply allow all that enters into your perception of reality to be as it is and take each moment as it comes. Be at one with the present moment, work diligently but only do what is needed in the moment, without strain.

## FORTY-FOUR

Fame or self: which matters more? Self or wealth: which is more precious? Gain or loss: which is more painful? He who is attached to things will suffer much. He who saves will suffer heavy loss. A contented man is never disappointed. He who knows when to stop does not find himself in trouble. He will stay forever safe.

**Interpretation**

Which is more important, to gain the material world and lose yourself, what would be more important to you, fame or being yourself? If you attach yourself to what is "out there" you will suffer a great loss, the greatest loss of all, losing yourself. Also, the balance of all things, and impermanence of all things, means to gain, you will eventually lose. Which is more painful? The struggle to gain? Or the loss after the gain? Perhaps both are painful, so why attach yourself to fame or wealth in the first place?

Someone who only seeks what is actually required, can be content once he or she has satisfied the need. One who knows when to stop, will not suffer any form of loss. This type of person will always be safe, because they will know who they are, and be content with the little they have.

## FORTY-FIVE

Great accomplishment seems imperfect, yet it does not outlive its usefulness. Great fullness seems empty, yet cannot be exhausted. Great straightness seems twisted. Great intelligence seems stupid. Great eloquence seems awkward. Movement overcomes cold. Stillness overcomes heat. Stillness and tranquility set things in order in the universe.

**Interpretation**

That which is a real accomplishment, may seem imperfect to those around, from an external perspective. The true accomplishments in this world, which one can achieve may seem strange, yet their usefulness remain. A man or woman, who is full, meaning someone who knows them self, and is content with less, may seem empty from an external viewpoint, yet their fullness is inexhaustible. To be one with the Tao, is great intelligence, yet seems stupid, because it means to let go of thinking. Great eloquence may seem stupid to some, because that which is generally accepted in society makes real knowledge out to be weird. These people favor silly things, like TV shows, Music videos, Magazines, Fashion, Cars, Jewelry, Shoes, Bags, Make up ETC. What is real is considered fake and vice versa.

To be still and at peace in the moment, is all that is required in the universe. It is the natural state of being.

## FORTY-SIX

When the Tao is present in the universe, the horses haul manure. When the Tao is absent from the universe, war horses are bred outside the city. There is no greater sin than desire, no greater curse than discontent, no greater misfortune than wanting something for oneself. Therefore he who knows that enough is enough will always have enough.

**Interpretation**

When one is at peace in each moment of reality, everything will run smoothly as it should. When one becomes out of sync with the present, chaos arises. There is no greater sin than desire. To desire creates all kinds of problems and confusion. To want something purely for selfish reasons is truly a misfortune and only creates further bewilderment and disorder.

The one who is content with what they have, will always be at peace and will create no more suffering for them self or others.

## FORTY-SEVEN

Without going outside, you may know the whole world. Without looking through the window, you may see the ways of heaven. The farther you go, the less you know. Thus the sage knows without traveling; he sees without looking; he works without doing.

**Interpretation**

You can hear of outside possessions, items, the egotistical positions of power, the endless pursuits of desire for materialism, yet you do not need to actually act upon what you know. In this world of bombardment, there is no escape from these things, which surround us at every corner of our lives. Without looking at these things you will be closer to the Tao. The further you go in to it yourself, the further closer to the Tao you become. The sage knows without participating, he sees these things and does not let them affect him/her, he or she does not act or react.

## FORTY-EIGHT

In the pursuit of learning, every day something is acquired. In the pursuit of Tao, every day something is dropped. Less and less is done until non-action is achieved. When nothing is done, nothing is left undone. The world is ruled by letting things take their course. It cannot be ruled by interfering.

**Interpretation**

In this era, what we call learning is to acquire from the outside realm and use this knowledge to further our progression in a man-made system. However to become closer to the Tao, we must endeavor to lose this knowledge bit by bit. Until we are no longer forcing a direction in our lives, and trying to become something we are not. When nothing is forced to be done, nothing can be incomplete. Let things take their course naturally without strain.

## FORTY-NINE

The sage has no mind of his own. He is aware of the needs of others. I am good to people who are good. I am also good to people who are not good. Because Virtue is goodness. I have faith in people who are faithful. I also have faith in people who are not faithful. Because Virtue is faithfulness. The sage is shy and humble - to the world he seems confusing. Others look to him and listen. He behaves like a little child.

**Interpretation**

The sage acts for others and not for himself, this allows him to feel truly rich inside. He is good to those who are good and to those who are bad, because the virtue of goodness has no preferences. If you are good - you are good! The sage is faithful to those who are faithful and unfaithful, because the virtue of faithfulness is a choice and not a reaction. The sage is shy and humble, he/she does not make him or herself obvious. To the world, he or she may not fit in. Others look and listen to him/her, because he/she behaves childlike, and they may find this strange. They wonder why he/she has no cares or worries.

## FIFTY

Between birth and death, three in ten are followers of life, three in ten are followers of death, and men just passing from birth to death also number three in ten. Why is this so? Because they live their lives on the gross level. He who knows how to live can walk abroad without fear of rhinoceros or tiger. He will not be wounded in battle. For in him rhinoceroses can find no place to thrust their horn, tigers no place to use their claws, and weapons no place to pierce. Why is this so? Because he has no place for death to enter.

**Interpretation**

A third of people, are actually living, a third are waiting to die (living in misery) and the final third believe they are living, yet they are merely part of the crowd, who simply pass from birth to death. The crowd who follow others and act in the exact same ways as those around them, are the ones who think following the crowd is true living. However those who truly know how to live, have no fear about what they do, because they know death is an illusion.

The present moment of reality is all there ever will be, and once the apparent future death comes (which will also be the present) it is only the body that passes. The true being underneath fades into the background. The body and the energy which gave you what you perceive as life, is still one with the Tao. Each moment of reality, is where living takes place.

One who knows how to live, knows how to use their moments wisely. As opposed to those, who fear or stress, who find life painful and wait for death to come. As opposed to those, who have no ability to be them self, and purely act like everyone around them - the crowd followers.

The one who knows how to live, does not fear what we call death, and simply does what feels right.

## FIFTY-ONE

All things arise from Tao. They are nourished by Virtue. They are formed from matter. They are shaped by environment. Thus the ten thousand things all respect Tao and honor Virtue. Respect of Tao and honor of Virtue are not demanded, but they are in the nature of things. Therefore all things arise from Tao. By Virtue they are nourished, developed, cared for, sheltered, comforted,grown, and protected. Creating without claiming, doing without taking credit, guiding without interfering, this is primal Virtue.

**Interpretation**

A tree does not grow in one day, the small acorn takes many years to become a mighty oak. All things are formed through the same substance as everything else, and are nourished by what is in closest proximity. Each natural thing in our awareness, flows effortlessly with the Tao, and honors the virtues of being one with the Tao. These virtues are not demanded in humans; and most believe they can act in a more graceful, elegant manner than all that naturally follows the Tao. This is the ignorance of Human Beings who do not follow the Tao.

Follow the Tao, and you will be nourished by virtue, you will develop slowly and securely (like the mighty oak) you will be sheltered from all negative thought forms, you will find comfort in the present; and will grow and feel protected. Simply be one with the Tao (the Present), work effortlessly, take no credit, guide but do not manipulate. These are the first virtues to develop.

## FIFTY-TWO

The beginning of the universe is the mother of all things. Knowing the mother, one also knows the sons. Knowing the sons, yet remaining in touch with the mother, brings freedom from the fear of death. Keep your mouth shut,guard the senses, and life is ever full. Open your mouth, always be busy,and life is beyond hope. Seeing the small is insight; yielding to force is strength. Using the outer light, return to insight, and in this way be saved from harm. This is learning constancy.

**Interpretation**

Knowing the origin of all things, one can see the manifestations. However knowing the origin, brings freedom and liberation from death, as one knows that they will only return to the source. Keep your mouth shut, means to speak little, as words create ripples like stones dropped in a lake. Be careful of what is said, once you say a word you cannot take it back. Guard your senses, do not allow them to be overwhelmed with the external reality. Stay close to the Tao and you will always be very full. Those that always seem to be in a rush to get somewhere; create new activities, and experience seek - will always be beyond hope. Yielding to force shows great strength, as force is a tool of evil. Stay pure and supple. Interpret the external world, yet return inside and find insight. In this way you will be protected from harm. Learn to stay faithful and dependable in these actions. That is Constancy.

## FIFTY-THREE

If I have even just a little sense, I will walk on the main road and my only fear will be of straying from it. Keeping to the main road is easy,but people love to be sidetracked. When the court is arrayed in splendor, the fields are full of weeds, and the granaries are bare. Some wear gorgeous clothes, carry sharp swords, and indulge themselves with food and drink; they have more possessions than they can use. They are robber barons. This is certainly not the way of Tao.

**Interpretation**

To stay one with the Tao, can be easy, but some people love to be sidetracked by things that sparkle. This could be, a night out drinking, partying, finding excitement in new experiences, shopping and spending money unnecessarily to name a few. When this takes over, the internal essence is being lost. It becomes hard to see the natural side of life. Those who indulge in extravagance, are far away from the Tao.

## FIFTY-FOUR

What is firmly established cannot be uprooted. What is firmly grasped cannot slip away. It will be honored from generation to generation. Cultivate Virtue in yourself, and Virtue will be real. Cultivate it in the family, and Virtue will abound. Cultivate it in the village, and Virtue will grow. Cultivate it in the nation, and Virtue will be abundant. Cultivate it in the universe,and Virtue will be everywhere. Therefore look at the body as body; look at the family as family; look at the village as village; look at the nation as nation; look at the universe as universe. How do I know the universe is like this? By looking!

**Interpretation**

That which is cultivated properly, cannot be taken away. Become fully virtuous and continually cultivate virtues in yourself and these virtues will never be lost. They can be passed down from generation to generation. Cultivate virtues in your family and the family will be virtuous. Extend these virtues to those around you, and the neighborhood becomes virtuous. If neighborhoods then lend their virtues to each other, the nation becomes virtuous. Cultivate it in the nation and virtues are abundant. Cultivate it everywhere and the universe is virtuous.

The Tao is truly virtuous, and it can be seen in anything natural if you look for it carefully.

## FIFTY-FIVE

He who is filled with Virtue is like a newborn child. Wasps and serpents will not sting him; wild beasts will not pounce upon him; he will not be attacked by birds of prey. His bones are soft, his muscles weak, but his grip is firm. He has not experienced the union of man and woman, but is whole. His manhood is strong. he screams all day without becoming hoarse. This is perfect harmony. Knowing harmony is constancy. Knowing constancy is enlightenment. It is not wise to rush about. Controlling the breath causes strain. If too much energy is used, exhaustion follows. This is not the way of Tao. Whatever is contrary to Tao will not last long.

## Interpretation

Become filled with virtue and return to your true nature, as you were when you were young. Before you clouded your internal psyche with vices. The virtuous are safe from harm, they will not be attacked. He or she appears soft, but is internally strong. The internal energy field is strong, like being celibate for years. He or she is whole, and resilient. Their energy is abundant. This is perfect harmony.

Knowing harmony is constancy, constancy is enlightenment. Rushing is for fools, holding the breath is unnatural and causes strain. If you use up too much energy doing unnatural things, you become exhausted, so it is best not to stress or strain.

The way of the Tao is natural and effortless. Whatever goes against it will not last long.

## FIFTY-SIX

Those who know do not talk. Those who talk do not know. Keep your mouth closed. Guard your senses. Temper your sharpness. Simplify your problems. Mask your brightness. Be at one with the dust of the Earth. This is primal union. He who has achieved this state Is unconcerned with friends and enemies, With good and harm, with honor and disgrace. This therefore is the highest state of man.

**Interpretation**

Those who know, that words power the intellectual thinking mind, don't speak, and those that speak do not know. Words cause the mind to wonder away from the present moment. Speaking and hearing language cause the mind to become split. It is the beginning of creating concepts in the mind, which take you further away from understanding and knowing the Tao, or being one with it, like everything in our reality which appears natural, (animals, tree's, birds, insects etc.).

In this existence with no escape from thinking, talking and listening, it is best to be simple in words and actions, do not appear to be too intellectual. Be modest in thought and action.

Become as close to the Tao as possible in this day and age, and you will be reunited with the source energy. One who achieves this state, will become less concerned with the external reality (friends, enemies, good and bad, honor or disgrace). He will not have any care or worries. This is the highest state to achieve.

## FIFTY-SEVEN

Rule a nation with justice. Wage war with surprise moves. Become master of the universe without striving. How do I know that this is so? Because of this! The more laws and restrictions there are, the poorer people become. The sharper men's weapons, the more trouble in the land. The more ingenious and clever men are, the more strange things happen. The more rules and regulations, the more thieves and robbers. Therefore the sage says: I take no action and people are reformed. I enjoy peace and people become honest. I do nothing and people become rich. I have no desires and people return to the good and simple life.

## Interpretation

If you govern a nation with fairness, all will be fine. Striving to control and there will be problems. The more laws and restrictions put in place, the poorer the people become, as they feel they have less options and cannot live their life properly. To rebel against laws and restrictions, the sharper the weapons become. More trouble arises to free themselves from the restrictions placed upon them. As the restrictions increase, people find cleverer ways to break free. Strange things happen, which are totally unforeseen.

With more restrictions come more thieves and robbers. The sage simply takes no action, and allows the people to be as they are, in this way they feel liberated and truly free. Be peaceful around people and find that they become honest. Give no restriction to them and they feel rich. Show them you desire less

for your own self, and the people around
follow your lead and return to a good and
simple life.

## FIFTY-EIGHT

When the country is ruled with a light hand the people are simple When the country is ruled with severity, the people are cunning. Happiness is rooted in misery. Misery lurks beneath happiness. Who knows what the future holds? There is no honesty. Honesty becomes dishonest. Goodness becomes witchcraft. Man's bewitchment lasts for a long time. Therefore the sage is sharp but not cutting, pointed but not piercing, straightforward but not unrestrained, brilliant but not blinding.

**Interpretation**

When leading anyone, lead with less restriction and subtle gestures. This way the people will have respect and follow. They will be simple and happy. To rule with an iron fist, causes rebellion. What appears happy, may have misery underneath! What might these people do in the future, to rebel against the underlying misery? What seems honest, may become dishonest. What appears as goodness becomes bad. The pain felt from rebellion will last a long time. Therefore the sage is direct, but not forceful, has good points but does not drive them in with a hammer, straightforward but doesn't overpower with words. Is bright but does not try to blind others. Let all things be as they are.

## FIFTY-NINE

In caring for others and serving heaven, there is nothing like using restraint. Restraint begins with giving up one's own ideas. This depends on Virtue gathered in the past. If there is a good store of Virtue, then nothing is impossible. If nothing is impossible, then there are no limits. If a man knows no limits, then he is fit to be a ruler. The mother principle of ruling holds good for a long time. This is called having deep roots and a firm foundation, the Tao of long life and eternal vision.

**Interpretation**

To restrain ones actions means to become less impulsive to control others and external circumstances. Giving up manipulating others to adopt your beliefs.

Lose the feeling to control the course of events!

Beliefs can be shown, but not forced on to others. This virtue is strengthened by continued use, and the more you use it the stronger it becomes. If your virtues are high, then nothing is impossible for you to achieve - there are no limits. With no limits you will be able to lead others. This principal of leading lasts a long time. It has deep roots like a tree which has grown with a solid foundation. Being virtuous like the Tao, gives long life to all and eternal vision.

## SIXTY

Ruling the country is like cooking a small fish, too much poking and you ruin it. Approach the universe with Tao, and evil is not powerful, its power will not be used to harm others. Not only will it do no harm to others, but the sage himself will also be protected. They do not hurt each other, and the Virtue in each one refreshes both.

**Interpretation**

To lead others, one should not try to use force or manipulate, this spoils things. Approach everything with virtues of the Tao and evilness has no power. There will be no evil to cause harm to others, and the sage him/herself will be protected. There will be no rebellion therefore they would not hurt each other. The virtue found in both refreshers each other.

## SIXTY-ONE

A great country is like low land. It is the meeting ground of the universe, the mother of the universe. The female overcomes the male with stillness,lying low in stillness. Therefore if a great country gives way to a smaller country, it will conquer the smaller country. And if a small country submits to a great country, it can conquer the great country. Therefore those who would conquer must yield, and those who conquer do so because they yield. A great nation needs more people; a small country needs to serve. Each gets what it wants. It is fitting for a great nation to yield.

**Interpretation**

The weak overcome the strong, that which is weak gives itself to the strong and then becomes stronger. That which is strong will conquer the weak, but the weak in other aspects will conquer the strong. They both get what they want. The weak and strong must yield to each other.

## SIXTY-TWO

Tao is the source of the ten thousand things. It is the treasure of the good man, and the refuge of the bad. Sweet words can buy honor; good deeds can gain respect. If a man is bad, do not abandon him. Therefore on the day the emperor is crowned, or the three officers of state installed, do not send a gift of jade and a team of FOUR horses, but remain still and offer the Tao. Why does everyone like the Tao so much at first? Isn't it because you find what you seek and are forgiven when you sin? Therefore this is the greatest treasure of the universe.

**Interpretation**

The Tao, offers peace for anyone, good or bad. Sweet words can buy you honor externally, and good deeds can gain respect. But the bad gain no respect in this world. However the Tao does not abandon the bad. It is a place of rest for both good and bad. The good revere it, the bad seek refuge in it. Do not offer gifts to others, simply guide them to the Tao, through your actions.

Once the Tao is discovered, everyone loves it, because you find what you seek (peace and happiness) and for those who are bad, you are forgiven for your sins. The Tao is the greatest treasure for anyone in the universe.

# SIXTY-THREE

Practice non-action. Work without doing. Taste the tasteless. Magnify the small, increase the few. Reward bitterness with care. See simplicity in the complicated. Achieve greatness in little things. In the universe the difficult things are done as if they are easy. In the universe great acts are made up of small deeds. The sage does not attempt anything very big, and thus achieves greatness. Easy promises make for little trust Taking things lightly results in great difficulty Because the sage always confronts difficulties, he never experiences them.

**Interpretation**

To achieve great accomplishments, do not seek to achieve instantly. Do not rush and expect to see results. Do not strain and force to get somewhere. Simply work slowly and diligently. Break it down in to very small manageable steps. Each of these small steps adds up over time and you will accomplish great things. All that is required is consistency, no matter how small the steps. Break it down in to pieces which are easy and effortless. Which is the practice of non-doing, working without doing. This literally means do not attempt the greatest of challenges, attempt the smallest of challenges one by one, until the great is accomplished. Be only concerned with the smaller action of the moment.

Do not make promises you cannot keep. Do not tie yourself to great achievements. Simply confront challenges as they come.

# SIXTY-FOUR

Peace is easily maintained; trouble is easily overcome before it starts. The brittle is easily shattered; the small is easily scattered. Deal with it before it happens. Set things in order before there is confusion. A tree as great as a man's embrace springs up from a small shoot; a terrace nine stories high begins with a pile of earth; a journey of a thousand miles starts under one's feet. He who acts defeats his own purpose; he who grasps loses The sage does not act, and so is not defeated. He does not grasp and therefore does not lose. People usually fail when they are on the verge of success. So give as much care to the end as to the beginning;then there will be no failure. Therefore the sage seeks freedom from desire. He does not collect precious things. He learns not to hold on to ideas

He brings men back to what they have lost. He helps the ten thousand things find their own nature, but refrains from action.

### Interpretation

Peace can be maintained, by following the virtues of the Tao, one can avoid trouble before it starts. Like throwing stones in a lake, which aggravate the water, once stones have stopped being thrown, the water will eventually settle again. We can maintain the peace and tranquility by not causing any more problems for ourselves and others.

One must endeavor to stay virtuous, because the longer these virtues are present in someone the stronger they become and the more peace we will find in our lives. If virtues are not present, when trying to be virtuous, it will be easy to fall off the path of the virtuous, because what is brittle is easily shattered and what is small is easily scattered. One must grow virtue like a tree, solid and strong with deep roots. A tree can be grown from a small seed, all that is required is persistence. Any journey begins with a step, but one must keep walking in the right direction.

These virtues must be rooted in your character, because one who acts goes against what they truly are, and one who grasps onto being something which they are not - will lose!

The sage does not act, so cannot lose who they are! Things like this must be slow and gradual. To try and be something we are not in a single day will not work, or last. Changes take a very long time, and should be natural and effortless.

People who are close to succeeding in change, give up just before they achieve great things, so give as much attention to the end as you do to the beginning - never give up. The only time you fail is when you give up - otherwise you cannot fail.

The sage seeks freedom from desire, because attaching to an external circumstance can only bring upset when it is not achieved. It is not wise to collect precious things, as when they are gone, one will not be happy. He/she does not act, they simply are one with all, and let things happen naturally as intended. This also shows others how to be, without acting to make them see.

## SIXTY-FIVE

In the beginning those who knew the Tao did not try to enlighten others, but kept it hidden. Why is it so hard to rule? Because people are so clever. Rulers who try to use cleverness cheat the country. Those who rule without cleverness are a blessing to the land. These are the two alternatives. Understanding these is Primal Virtue. Primal Virtue is deep and far. It leads all things back toward the great oneness.

**Interpretation**

Those that are one with the Tao, try not to force enlightenment onto others, they keep it hidden, but visible in their presence and actions. Those that try to rule others through cleverness will find it difficult to find followers. Those that use no cleverness are revered by all. Understanding the difference here is a virtue, which has deep roots. Understanding it leads all people back to oneness.

## SIXTY-SIX

Why is the sea king of a hundred streams? Because it lies below them. Therefore it is the king of a hundred streams. If the sage would guide the people, he must serve with humility. If he would lead them, he must follow behind. In this way when the sage rules, the people will not feel oppressed; when he stands before them, they will not be harmed. The whole world will support him and will not tire of him. Because he does not compete, he does not meet competition.

**Interpretation**

All streams come back to the sea, because the sea is lower. Therefore the sage stays behind all, yet they all return to him/her. The sage leads from behind, this way the people do not feel they are being led, or restricted. When the sage stands before the people, they will have respect for him/her and do not get tired of the sage's wisdom. The sage guides with humility and stands behind others. Letting them be free with only simple actions to guide their steps.

The sage does not compete with anyone, therefore there is no competition.

## SIXTY-SEVEN

Everyone under heaven says that my Tao is great and beyond comparison. Because it is great, it seems different.If it were not different, it would have vanished long ago. I have three treasures which I hold and keep. The first is mercy; the second is economy; the third is daring not to be ahead of others. From mercy comes courage; from economy comes generosity; from humility comes leadership. Nowadays men shun mercy, but try to be brave; they abandon economy, but try to be generous; they do not believe in humility, but always try to be first. This is certain death. Mercy brings victory in battle and strength in defense. It is the means by which heaven saves and guards.

## Interpretation

Everyone who understands the Tao, knows the Tao does not compare to anything else. Because it is great once it has been found, it stands out. If it were not different it would of vanished (it cannot die).

There are three treasures, one is mercy, the second economy, and the third not trying to be ahead of others. When one asks for forgiveness they actually show courage, and once they renounce their sins, they can be clear minded and form courage. From being economical, one can be generous, in thoughts and actions, not just monetary. Being humble and not trying to compete and be ahead - one can lead.

Some try to be brave without asking for mercy for anything, any forgiveness. Some are not economical yet want to be generous, however this is only going to cause problems, because they cannot continuously be generous. And some do not believe in humility but always want to be first. This will only stir up negative feelings towards them in others. Not holding on to mercy, economy and humility brings negative outcomes.

Mercy brings victory when battling. The one who yields to overcome is stronger. Mercy protects and saves one from harm.

## SIXTY-EIGHT

A good soldier is not violent. A good fighter is not angry. A good winner is not vengeful. A good employer is humble. This is known as the Virtue of not striving. This is known as ability to deal with people. This since ancient times has been known as the ultimate unity with heaven.

**Interpretation**

One who is strong is not violent. They hold immense inner strength and do not need to display force externally, they have nothing to prove. Their inner strength is more important to them. One who is internally strong, is not angry because he knows he can use another's angry energy against them self and let them cause their own self destruction. Someone who wins, never wins through being vengeful. To employ others one must be humble. To know these virtues, is to understand that there is no striving to achieve. They are simply being as peaceful as possible and this is the greatest victory. No achievement ever comes from being un-peaceful. Being peaceful is the ultimate unity with the Tao.

## SIXTY-NINE

There is a saying among soldiers: I dare not make the first move but would rather play the guest; I dare not advance and inch but would rather withdraw a foot. This is called marching without appearing to move, rolling up your sleeves without showing your arm,capturing the enemy without attacking,being armed without weapons. There is no greater catastrophe than underestimating the enemy. By underestimating the enemy, I almost lost what I value. Therefore when the battle is joined, the underdog will win.

### Interpretation

In life one should not create battles. The one who starts the war, will lose internally. They can win externally - this may be a victory which has caused mass destruction and the loss of many lives. But they create no good and only self-harm by creating this type of atmosphere.

The true winner, responds to those that create a war by retreating - the true winner does not want to fight. This is to capture and win without attacking. Let the enemy cause their own self destruction, without losing any of your energy.

To create a war and underestimate what the other can do, is the catastrophe, therefore it is not wise to start a war with anyone, or a war against the Tao, you will lose. The underdog, the one who does not create wars and retreats when one has been started is always safe.

## SEVENTY

My words are easy to understand and easy to perform, yet no man under heaven knows them or practices them. My words have ancient beginnings. My actions are disciplined. Because men do not understand, they have no knowledge of me. Those that know me are few; those that abuse me are honored. Therefore the sage wears rough clothing and holds the jewel in his heart.

## Interpretation

Although these words are easy to understand, and it is simple to become one with the Tao, not many perform the actions, or chose to be one with the Tao. They see the external world and are drawn into it. Although the Tao is disciplined, those around do not notice it because they do not understand. Those that do understand - are few; and those that abuse the Tao feel honored by the things they collect or experience from the external environment.

The true sage, disregards the external world, wears shabby clothes, because the true jewels and held internally.

## SEVENTY-ONE

Knowing ignorance is strength. Ignoring knowledge is sickness. If one is sick of sickness, then one is not sick. The sage is not sick because he is sick of sickness. Therefore he is not sick.

**Interpretation**

To know the ignorance of others, or oneself, is the beginning of true understanding and strength. If you are tired of your own or others sickness, then you are becoming well. The sage is sick of the sickness he sees around him, therefore he is not sick.

This world tries to draw people into a weird fantasy, which has a never ending pursuit for happiness in external objects and materialism, this is the sickness of the world, which has been created by media and social culture. Once this has been realized, one can start to heal. To understand the sickness of the world, is to finally not be sick yourself.

## SEVENTY-TWO

When men lack a sense of awe, there will be disaster. Do not intrude in their homes. Do not harass them at work. If you do not interfere, they will not be weary of you. Therefore the sage knows himself but makes no show, has self-respect but is not arrogant. He lets go of that and chooses this.

**Interpretation**

When you no longer see the beauty of the world around you start to become sick, this causes disaster. There is so much wonder in the world, which can be found in nature, yet many ignore the truth and seek the fake in the material world. This leads to internal disaster and conflict.

Do not intrude in others minds or where they dwell, do not harass others or interfere with their lives then no one will be weary of you. The sage knows to have self-respect and makes no show. He has no arrogance and doesn't try to force his/her opinions on others. This way no one becomes weary of him/her. He lets go of intrusion and chooses to be humble.

## SEVENTY-THREE

A brave and passionate man will kill or be killed. A brave and calm man will always preserve life. Of these two which is good and which is harmful? Some things are not favored by heaven. Who knows why? Even the sage is unsure of this. The Tao of heaven does not strive, and yet it overcomes. It does not speak, and yet is answered. It does not ask, yet is supplied with all its needs. It seems to have no aim and yet its purpose is fulfilled. Heaven's net casts wide. Though its meshes are course, nothing slips through.

**Interpretation**

Someone who is brave to try but has extreme passions will only cause problems for either others, or himself/herself. However someone who is brave, but calm, always preserves life, for others and him/herself. Extreme passion goes against the Tao, to be calm is to work towards a purpose naturally without seeking to win, or compete with others. Striving to achieve, either uses up your energy quickly, or steps on others to get where you are trying to go.

Harm to yourself or others is not favored by the Tao. The Tao does not strive in this manner, yet every purpose is achieved. It does not unnaturally speak yet can be answered. It does not have to ask for anything, yet everything is provided.

Follow a purpose without straining and everything will become abundant, all will be achieved slowly and effortlessly, without strain, and without causing harm to yourself and others.

The Tao's meshes are course, means nothing leaves the Tao, all is one.

## SEVENTY-FOUR

If men are not afraid to die, It is no avail to threaten them with death. If men live in constant fear of dying, and if breaking the law means that a man will be killed, who will dare to break the law? There is always an official executioner. If you try to take his place, it is like trying to be a master carpenter and cutting wood. If you try to cut wood like a master carpenter, you will only hurt your hand.

## Interpretation

If people are not afraid to die, they can act in the present however they want, because the greatest fear of humans is death. If they are not scared of death, then they can do as they want and not fear anything. If they are scared they will not act, they will not dare to try anything.

Humanity is suppressed by the fear of being themselves, because there are too many rules and restrictions which have been placed on the mind. The official executioners are the puppet masters who control the world, if you were to try take their place and control the people you will fail. You cannot be something you are not. To try and be something else, which does not come naturally will only backfire.

## SEVENTY-FIVE

Why are the people starving? Because the rulers eat up the money in taxes. Therefore the people are starving. Why are the people rebellious? Because the rulers interfere too much. Therefore they are rebellious. Why do the people think so little of death? Because the rulers demand too much of life. Therefore the people take death lightly. Having little to live on, one knows better than to value life too much.

**Interpretation**

The people are suffering because the rulers keep them in oppression, they eat up all the resources and take the little the people have. The people become rebellious because of these restrictions, and resent the interference of the rulers.

The people do not contemplate death much because the rulers demand too much of their life, and do not give them time contemplate existence.

To contemplate death is to acknowledge death, and understand that all of the external world is not real and to appreciate life while we are here. One can only value the little life they have, when they have time to enjoy being natural. Mainly in this life now, it is almost impossible to relax, and enjoy life, because the demands on the people are extremely heavy.

## SEVENTY-SIX

A man is born gentle and weak. At his death he is hard and stiff. Green plants are tender and filled with sap. At their death they are withered and dry. Therefore the stiff and unbending is the disciple of death. The gentle and yielding is the disciple of life. Thus an army without flexibility never wins a battle. A tree that is unbending is easily broken. The hard and strong will fall.The soft and weak will overcome.

**Interpretation**

What is supple has life, those that can relax and stay stress free live long lives. They are full of life energy and it flows freely. Those that become wound up by the external world, become lifeless internally and start to develop stiffness and inflexibility. This is the nature of the dead, the lifeless. That which is inflexible and unyielding is not alive. The soft and yielding has life, and lives long. This is why an army without flexibility never wins, a stiff tree snaps in the wind. The hard and strong will fail, the soft and weak will overcome.

Be soft and flexible in the mind - and the body relaxes. Relax the body, and the mind becomes calm. Work on both, to become completely supple and yield to the Tao.

## SEVENTY-SEVEN

The Tao of heaven is like the bending of a bow. The high is lowered, and the low is raised. If the string is too long, it is shortened; If there is not enough, it is made longer. The Tao of heaven is to take from those who have too much and give to those who do not have enough. Man's way is different. He takes from those who do not have enough and give to those who already have too much. What man has more than enough and gives it to the world? Only the man of Tao. Therefore the sage works without recognition. He achieves what has to be done without dwelling on it. He does not try to show his knowledge.

## Interpretation

The Tao always aims to balance, and brings all things into harmony and synchronicity with each other. That which goes up, will come down, and that which is down will go up. It gives to that which has little, and takes from that which has a lot.

The men and women of this world, want to take from those who have little and give to those who have a lot. This goes against the Tao. The one who has a lot and gives, is in line with the Tao.

The sage, simply aims to be in the middle. He does not seek to have too much or too little. He achieves only what is needed and does not dwell on it. He does not show off, because those that show off, will lose what they have. Simply stay in the middle.

## SEVENTY-EIGHT

Under heaven nothing is more soft and yielding than water. Yet for attacking the solid and strong, nothing is better; it has no equal. The weak can overcome the strong; the supple can overcome the stiff. Under heaven everyone knows this, yet no one puts it into practice. Therefore the sage says: he who takes upon himself the humiliation of the people is fit to rule them. He who takes upon himself the country's disasters deserves to be king of the universe. The truth often sounds paradoxical.

**Interpretation**

Nothing is stronger than the soft, in all senses. The soft yield and protect themselves from harm, they also have life energy freely flowing internally. Those which are solid and stiff are weak internally and are compensating for something. The truth seems paradoxical, because externally what seems strong is not true strength. The one who is soft and weak is strong, yet no one puts this into practice. He who takes the blows of others and continues, is stronger than them, for being able to absorb the pain, while the other gains some form of gratification internally, this is only masking their weakness. The one who can handle the disasters of a nation deserves to be the king.

## SEVENTY-NINE

After a bitter quarrel, some resentment must remain. What can one do about it? Therefore the sage keeps his half of the bargain but does not exact his due. A man of Virtue performs his part,but a man without Virtue requires others to fulfill their obligations. The Tao of heaven is impartial.It stays with good men all the time.

**Interpretation**

After an argument some resentment may remain, but what can you do about it? The sage will always uphold his part of the settlement, the compromise. But does not expect anything from the other. Because the virtuous man/woman sticks to their word, whether or not the other does. The un-virtuous person, only seeks what the other will do for them and does not care to change. The Tao is impartial, however it will always be close to those that are good and with virtue.

# EIGHTY

A small country has fewer people. Though there are machines that can work ten to a hundred times faster than man, they are not needed. The people take death seriously and do not travel far. Though they have boats and carriages, no one uses them. Though they have armor and weapons, no one displays them. Men return to the knotting of rope in place of writing. Their food is plain and good, their clothes fine but simple, their homes secure; they are happy in their ways. Though they live within sight of their neighbors, and crowing cocks and barking dogs are heard across the way, yet they leave each other in peace while they grow old and die.

## Interpretation

A small country may have a few people, and although there are machines in this world that can work hundreds of times faster than the people, no one wants to use them, they are not needed. The people who contemplate death, wish to truly live without losing their core being, to the external man made artificial world. Though there is such thing as weapons of harm, no one wants to use them, they do not believe in harm and creating problems.

The people of the Tao, return to performing natural actions, without too many words and cleverness. They eat simple but good food, wear fine clothes which are simple. Their homes are unthreatened. And because no one seeks anything externally there are no thieves and robbers. They are happy with a simple life, they leave each other in peace and slowly grow old and die gracefully.

# EIGHTY-ONE

Truthful words are not beautiful. Beautiful words are not truthful. Good men do not argue. Those who argue are not good. Those who know are not learned. The learned do not know. The sage never tries to store things up. The more he does for others, the more he has. The more he gives to others, the greater his abundance. The Tao of heaven is pointed but does no harm. The Tao of the sage is work without effort.

## Interpretation

The truth does not point to a fantasy world, which asks people to find happiness in the future, in arriving at a destination, or acquiring external possessions. The truth may be painful for some, it may hurt, and it is not widely considered as beautiful, however the truth which is the Tao, is the true beauty of the world.

A good man causes no argument, those who cause arguments are not good. The good know there is nothing good in creating arguments and have no need for them. The bad create arguments for no reason, and this only causes problems for themselves and others.

Those that know the truth, are not men or women of the knowledge based world, they are one with the Tao. Those who are of worldly external knowledge do not truly know. Their mind is full of words and thoughts and not one with the Tao.

The sage does not hoard external objects, the more he/she gives away the more he/she has internally. They create happiness for those around them and themselves, and the more he/she will receive in the future to then give away. The Tao is pointed, very straight forward, but does not harm anything. The sage is the same, he/she holds the values of the Tao and does not harm. They both work without effort.

# FOR MORE ADAPTED CLASSICS PLEASE VISIT:

HTTP://VIEWAUTHOR.AT/JAMESHARRIS

## END